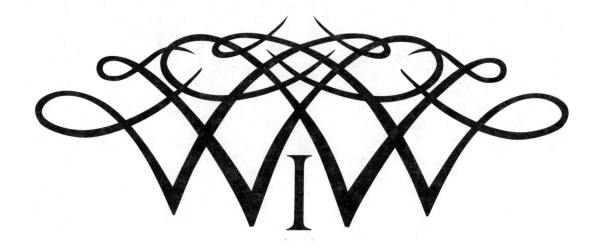

Walking In Williamsburg

Gray Nelson Oliver

Author
Gray Nelson Oliver

Publisher
Wayne Dementi
Dementi Milestone Publishing, Inc.
Manakin-Sabot, VA 23103
www.dementimilestonepublishing.com

Cataloging-in-publication data for this book is available from
The Library of Congress.
ISBN: 978-1-7368989-9-4

Graphic design by:
Jayne E. Hushen
Dementi Milestone Publishing, Inc.

Printed in the USA

DEDICATION

There are no better friends, mentors, leaders, and exemplars than my mother and father, Sharon and Albert Oliver. Their loving and caring relationship for each other and for each of us as children is grounded in faith, support, commitment, and the belief that with God all things are possible. Their deep and abiding love has withstood the test of time, standing today as a model of a lifetime commitment for us all. They constantly gave of themselves to us sons, Albert III, Gray and Erick,-and to our ever-widening circle of family and friends, as we grew from boys to men, in an idyllic west end Richmond neighborhood called Farmington.

I am truly grateful for the gift of my wife Cynthia and the love that we have shared over the decades, and that continues to grow with each passing day. Her loving and caring ways have formed the foundation of our family. As "Mom" to Keysin, Nelson, Connor and Trenor. She has given all of our children (and me) the power to "think big" and to "dare to do great things".

Finally, I owe a great debt to my favorite aunt Genevieve and uncle Stuart Hughes, lifetime residents of Williamsburg, and to my cousins Stuart and Susan. The times we spent at their home on 106 Newport Avenue and aboard The Excalibur (moored at Queen's Creek) will be with me and my family forever. There is no equal to summer in Williamsburg surrounded by a large and loving family.

COLONIAL QUILL

PRESS & PUBLISHING

8900 THREE CHOPT ROAD, RICHMOND, VIRGINIA, 27029

PREFACE

Many of us have sacred places that we return to throughout our lives that serve as both anchors and crucibles. Some that exist physically and some that are forever etched in our minds.

Sacred places, that both form our foundation of self while also helping us burn off the non-essential baggage we accumulate in life that may be holding us back, or is of limited or no value to us.

Williamsburg is such a place for me. Over my life, I have both visited and lived in Williamsburg virtually every year of my life. In fact, my life began in Williamsburg when my parents, Albert and Sharon, welcomed their second son, while my dad finished his degree at The College of William and Mary. From that day on, I have been making annual sabbaticals to this place where my life began and will likely end. I've also had the blessing of living in Williamsburg in four different and distinct phases of my life (as a teen, as a student at W&M, as a young professional, and in middle age), leading me to the title of this work.

It is against this backdrop that this offering, Walking in Williamsburg originates. Not surprisingly, my first attempts at creative writing and poetry were completed while on campus at W&M in the late 1970s, in the Christopher Wren building where Thomas Jefferson is reported to have passed English 101 and Introduction to Creative Writing, and we all know where that story ended.

From there, as my adult life began, I wrote "in the moment" capturing the fiction and the non-fiction happenings in my life at the time that I had either observed, experienced or imagined. As you read each poem, I'll leave it to you, the reader, to wonder as to my source of inspiration, perspiration, confuscation, or to the veracity of each tale. Owing to the advent of the computer and hard drive, I archived these works through the decades and now share them in hopes the reader may find some of the hope, joy, fun, pain, power, redemption and forgiveness that I found in penning them, and maybe in the process save a few dollars in therapy fees.

To me, Williamsburg has always been a sacred and historic place. A place where our centuries old history as a country began to be formed.

A place where our democracy was conceived and through its infancy grew to take its first steps onto the world stage. Today, you can close your eyes on Duke of Gloucester street in front of the House of Burgesses and be transported back to the heated arguments that led to the decision to separate from our Mother Country, Great Britain. Or, listen for the raised voices at Chowning's Tavern as the early Patriots hotly debated our governmental structure, fueled by more than a few mugs of ale. These historic places are all still there, many unchanged, by the more than three centuries that have passed.

Come…walk with me,
as I have walked through the years,
through the laughter and the tears,
waking, working, wasted, occasionally weeping,
always wondering in Williamsburg…

Gray Nelson Oliver

gnotsm@gmail.com | 804-350-1689

∾ Weeping In Williamsburg ∾

∾ Wondering In Williamsburg ∾

Waking
In
Williamsburg

Circles

We come into community from family to friends,
Learning from all we touch, expanding until the end.
Friends raise us up, in a world that puts us down,
Searching for a life path, as the world spins round.
In our hearts, we are all the same.
No need to sweat it, it's all in the game.

Imaginary boundaries, drawn to separate us all,
No real distinctions, kingdoms rise and fall.
Media screaming loudly, seeking to divide,
Don't care what happens to you, as long as I get mine.
In our hearts, we're all the same.
Ignore what you hear, delete or go insane.

Six billion souls - - - of one mind,
Reaching for the spirit, leaving the past behind.
See the beauty that abounds, with eyes open wide,
All the energy we ever need, surrounds us on all sides.
In our hearts, we're all the same,
How do we stop the burn, in a world that's aflame?

Spinning through space, destinations yet unknown,
Guided by our faith, seeds of future sewn.
In our hearts, we're all the same,
Listen closely, the Universe is calling your name.

Forsake

The eyes they see, the mind it measures.
The world surrounds, with earthly pleasures.
The ears they hear, the notes of our life.
A symphony of love and pain, amid joy and strife.

There are chances that we take,
There are smiles that we fake.
There are choices that me make,
There are lives that we forsake.

The mouth it speaks, it can raise or cut.
Leave them better than you found them, or keep it shut.
The head it thinks, what place do I have.
A universe so big, what things can I grab.

The heart it feels, colors of the rainbow.
The number of beats, no one can ever know.
What determines if we stay, who shall cause us to depart.
Others stand in stillness, a matter of the heart.

Who in our lives do we forsake?
Is it our role to give, or to take?
Shall we raise them up, or cut them as they fall?
This my friend is the hardest question of all....

Invisible

Invisible, the world can barely see,
The fire that burns so brightly in me.

People walking by, none of them speak,
Non-caring souls, not knowing what they seek.

Paced by their friends, chasing the dollar,
Bigger the house, tighter the collar.

Clothes make the man, painted on smiles,
They're naked inside, it's all about style.
Action without intent, absent the heart,
Damages the soul, tears people apart.

Emotional amputation, where shall I cut,
Words are my knife, I can't shut up.
Blood on the floor, who will survive?
Society is waiting, sharpening the knives.

Should you walk on, or turn and run away,
It's someone else's game, why should you play?
Surrender the knife, seek stillness instead,
Unleash the fire burning brightly inside your head.

Consuming all and gone in a flash,
Dormant not dead, life reborn in the ash.
Visible, now the world can clearly see,
The fire that burns so brightly in me.

Stop Waiting for Signs

Come out of the darkness, step into the light,
Not all of our choices, turn out to be right.

> Some days we are blind, wishing for sight,
> Floating, drifting, in the stream of life.

The days rush by, never to return,
Memories remain, and a few lessons learned.

> Tomorrows not here, comes in its own time,
> Don't misuse the present, stop waiting for signs.

Look for your passion, what makes your heart leap,
Open your eyes, what world do you seek?

> All you have seen, just tapes in your head,
> Waiting to be burned, just start again.

The joy is in loving, so give in each day,
See the best in others, it is God's way.

> Give from your heart in everything you do,
> And the world will always smile back at you.

Tomorrows not here, comes in its own time,
Don't misuse the present, stop waiting for signs.

Divine Stillness

When a moment becomes a lifetime, and failure is afoot.

Society, it tracks us, puts us to the boot.

Measure happens daily, as silent as the sun.

The scorching heat of life, soon the give-up comes.

Yet the sun it soon rises, new day indeed.

Machine it keeps grinding, driving Man onto his knees.

Which of us are buyers, we all have nothing to sell.

Sweat dropping off our brow, broken hands that swell.

But with hearts still beating strong,

Standing against the tide.

Minds rejecting the golden calf,

Seeking humility not pride.

In the quiet stillness of knowing,

The Divine is found.

Man becomes the mountain,

Standing high above the clouds.

Lose Yourself

In your teens it's about the women,
Cars that you drive.
Brothers and the beer,
Belonging to the Tribe.

College is about knowledge,
Your boundaries expand,
Lifelong friends will gather,
Staying with you until the end.
     One day you'll lose yourself in love,
     Along the road you'll find a girl,
     In time she'll be your friend.
     Becoming one in the end.

From this one will come many,
Blends of different parts.
Love is compounding,
An expansion of the heart
     Time passes quickly,
     Days string into years.
     Last child dropped at college,
     Can't hold back the tears.

The house suddenly empty
Kids long gone, don't call.
There's a silence in the home,
No footsteps down the hall.
     Along the road, you found a soul,
     Who became your best friend.
     A sharing spirit committed in love,
     Together until the end.

Empty Chairs

The basement door swings open, smoke hanging in the air.
The whole bar is jammed, not a single empty chair.
The local sports legends, they gather every year.
To share all their old stories, and have a few beers.

In their 50's they were rolling, smoking cigs by the pack.
Knocking drinks back like water, and never looking back.
Now the circle gets smaller, with each passing year.
Friends and brothers falling fast, leaving the empty chair.

In their 60's they were slowing, early years took a toll.
Backs and knees now failing, their steps begin to slow.
In their 70's they're shrinking, even the biggest now look small.
Hair gray with deep lined smiles, familiar faces they can't recall.

Now the door swings open, all you see are empty chairs.
There's an air of respect, remembering those no longer there.
The circle gets smaller, with each passing year.
Friends and brothers falling fast, leaving the empty chair.

Now they start each gathering, with the names lost that year.
The brothers listen in silence, grief too much to bear.
They look around in silence, eyes moving from face to face.
Wondering who among them, will not return to this place.

Faces now grown tired, muscles long since melted away,
But once a year they gather, all are heroes on this day.

This poem is dedicated to all the Richmond area athletes that participated in what during the 1940's/1950's/1960's where arch-rival, year making football games played around the Thanksgiving Holiday at City Stadium. These games featured crosstown rivals who battled for annual "bragging rights". Both of these games would consistently draw between 20,000-30,000 alumni and fans. These "Classics" featured Armstrong High vs. Maggie L. Walker High, and Thomas Jefferson High vs. John Marshall High, with the James river as the separating line.

One Last Throw

I never knew my grandad,
 died before my birth.
My Dad had lost his father,
God knows that must have hurt.

He was only seventeen,
when Big Al passed away.
He pitched a winning baseball game,
buried his Father the next day.
If I'd known that you were leaving,
We'd have had just one last throw.
Cause you taught me how to play,
And your love helped me grow.

In his hand they placed a ball,
signed by all the team.
Resting softly in his palm,
his fingers wrapped the seams.

When that casket closed,
My father became a man.
Now his memories are all he had,
Of his father's steady hand.
 For my grandad was a big man,
in death we all look small.
But through my dad he lives on,
 in the love dad gave us all.
If I'd known that you were leaving,
We'd have had just one last throw.
Cause you taught me how to play,
And your love helped me grow.

A Moment Of Love

A moment seems,
A hard thing to live,
In it remember,
You get what you give.

    A closed mind,
    Creates a hardened heart,
    Living in love,
    Creates a world apart.

A minute links,
Thought to act,
The chance of connection,
A life reset.

A lifetime of love,
With no regrets,
The giver of love,
No one forgets.

    A closed mind,
    Creates a hardened heart,
    Living in love,
    Let's make a new start.

A lifetime of love,
With no regrets,
The giver of love,
No one forgets.

You've Always Known

Two types of souls,
    Those who meet distress and dissonance,
    Those who use distress to find their essence.

    The silenced, strangled, muted voice, ready to roar,
    Neglected, ignored by society,
    Trampled by the hoard.

    Bleeding, wounded, but still aware,
    A soul entrapped, but no one cares,
    Save a knowing God...that's always there.

    Calm the soul, reach out your hand,
    Come off your knees,
    I'll help you stand.

    Union restored, united we are,
    I've always been here, never far.
    In stillness you have always known,
    I've always been your own.

Hearts Melding

I never knew a moment, could change a man's life.
A pretty woman smiles, soon to be his wife.

Started as friends, soon to be lovers.
The sacred gift of soul, like no other.

>That look in the moment,
>The smile is the start,
>The joining of hands,
>The melding of hearts.

The shared path chosen, a new world in bloom,
Two becoming one, from alter to tomb.

Rejoicing in love, embracing through pain.
Walking hills and valleys, a love sustained.

>That look in the moment,
>The smile is the start,
>The joining of hands,
>The melding of hearts.

Joined together, wherever the path goes.
Our love grows daily, in the kindness we show.

>A look in the moment,
>The smile is the start,
>The joining of hands,
>The melding of hearts.

A Blind Date In Buckhead*

It can happen in an instant,
Our world turned upside down,
All things suddenly possible,
A love now found.

A surprise birthday party,
My one and only blind date,
Only later would I see,
It was the hand of fate.

My mom taught me manners,
A friend of a friend,
Went south from the first moment,
Could not wait for it to end.
On entering the party,
In the land of the Georgia peach,
Southern drawls were heavy,
Don't be fooled by the speech.

She sat in a corner,
Talking with the honored guest,
Dressed to the nines,
Couldn't help but be impressed.

A pink and green flowered print,
In keeping with the times,
Polos here, preppies back,
The 60s' back in style.

A stately southern beauty,

Standing five foot twelve,

An easy confident manner,

I was instantly under her spell.

While courtesy was called for,

Opportunity could not be missed,

The doors of fate wide open,

I hastened, careful not to trip.

I made my introduction,

A lifetime started with a word,

Lost forever in time,

It surely must have worked.

Now 40 years later,

It's easy to return to that day,

That springtime birthday party,

My life would never be the same.

It's truly amazing how our lives,

Can be forever changed in an instant.

One moment we never saw coming,

One person we weren't looking for.

One love that changed everything,

One life now full of unimaginable possibilities.

---

*In the late 70's and early 80's many a romance was started in Buckhead, against the backdrop of beach music and Budweiser. Few knew that Buckhead had been a legendary, almost mythical "party district" since Henry Irby established Buckhead Tavern in the 1840's. In the 70's and 80's the bar name had changed --- Harrison's, Buckhead Beach, Johnny's Hideaway. Cross sections of college graduates for schools all over the southeast moved to Atlanta, forgetting about school loyalties, and now in a full headlong pursuit of the perfect mate, or maybe just a fun night out on the town, your call.

You Are The World To Me

I've searched the world over,

Climbing mountains high, sailing stormy seas,

Journeyed over a million miles,

In search of a world that could be.

True love is found in actions,

Some clear, some harder to see,

In the joining of our spirits,

You opened up a new world to me.

Gentle is your touch, a smile so sweet,

A world about to change, on the day we would meet.

Who sets the spark of life?

Surely love surrounds the seed,

A love newly sprouted,

A future ours to seek.

Gentle is your touch,

a smile so sweet,

A new world,

 ours to seek.

Hearts now soaring,

Dreaming of what will be.

Possibilities unlimited,

As long as you're with me.

A smile so sweet

A new world we can see.

A smile so sweet

A world yet to be.

Spokes in the Wheel

When the shadows crowd us all,
When the sky seems about to fall,
The noise exploding loud and raw,
Wishing I could hear your call.

A voice, a lifeline from the deep,
A heart once given, I'll always keep,
Together, we could calm the noise,
Bodies joined, it's our choice.

We are all spokes in the wheel,
Work units, put to the heel,
Unplug your head, use your hands,
When will you make a stand?

Walled against the world outside,
Spirits joined, together we'd ride,
In search of love that's missed,
Opened up with our first kiss.

Hold me like you'll never let go,
My thoughts you have always known,
Two are lost, there is only one,
Union with our God is done.

We are all spokes in the wheel,
Spinning, trying not to feel,
The gears grinding in our heart,
Call us to make another start.

Nature spins, spokes in the wheel,
Mind must know, body feel.
Two souls adrift, now at rest,
In finding you, I've been blessed.

Lake Toxaway Sunrise

As the crickets chirped and the crows cawed,
Night yielded to day, and time paused.

Waves of daylight, bleaching the night sky,
The crescent Moon, calling the Sun to rise.

First rays of the day, break over oak and pine,
Dancing across the lake, a road to the divine.

Surrounded in warmth, the Sun fully risen,
Day now begins, darkness giving way to vision.

What shall you do? In this day you have been given,
Act through your faith, your sins are forgiven.

Love those around you, some you've yet to meet,
Be a light unto others, be the peace that you seek.

A Son fully risen, shares limitless rays,
Bringing warmth to all, for all of His days.

The Water's Edge

I have breached the water's edge,
Where pine and oak dare not tread,
Nearly naked, gray and worn,
Reaching for the sky, water born.

Barren nubs, unfinished starts,
Mother Nature reaching out, retracing the heart,
Branches sprout, not reaching far,
Green means life- - -we grow, we are.

Living in water, rooted in the land,
Seeking the Sun, the Trinity of Man,
Seek the God in all who you meet,
The CEO, the pastor, the beggar on the street.

The Father, the Son, the Holy Ghost,
Water, land, daily rays of hope,
Take time to conceive, more to create,
Dream the future into today.

We all return to where we began,
On the path to becoming a spiritual man,
Walk as a light for all to see,
For ours is a World sorely in need.

Enter the water,
Come swim with me,
The rippling waves,
The gentle river breeze.

Get quiet each day,
Returning to your source,
Knowing your center,
Will straighten your course.

I have breached the water's edge,
Where pine and oak dare not tread.

Working
In
Williamsburg

Risk We Take

What makes you happy,
What makes you sing?
Do you collect people,
Or do you collect things?

Give yourself away,
Every chance you get,
Moment by moment,
With no regrets.

A twist to the dial,
A quirk of fate,
A random chance,
The risk we take.

Your path will clear,
The clouds will lift,
Your time and energy,
Is your greatest gift.

A twist to the dial,
A quirk of fate,
A Random Chance,
The risk we take.

The Water Line

Floating along the stream of life,
I'm all smiles, but can't mask the strife.
Without any notice, I'm over the falls,
Before I hit bottom, I've lost it all.

    The same things you need to float,
    Can surely one day drown you.

I'm just above the water line,
Treading water, arms weary.
Gasping for air, each time I surface,
Reaching for help…no one's there.

    Don't hold on to things too tight,
    Be careful who surrounds you.
    The same people who are helping you float,
    May surely, one day drown you.

I'm sinking below the water line,
Might bob up one more time.
Dreaming of days when all was fine,
Before the world crushed my mind.
Just below the surface,
Under the water line,
Between what you know and what you don't
You'll find your peace of mind.

    Don't hold on to things too tight,
    Be careful who surrounds you.
    The same people offering the helping hand,
    Will surely, one day drown you.

Some Days

Is there a difference,
Between one day and the next?
One, full of surprises,
The other, only what you expect.

The promise of the sun rise,
Followed by the closing sunset.
Some days filled with love,
Some days filled with neglect.

No one knows,
What the day may bring.
The people you'll meet,
May make your heart sing.
The world is waiting,
What shall you do?
Some days it's all others,
Some days it's all you.

Unimaginable feats,
Draw the world's applause.
Unthinkable acts,
Giving mankind pause.
        Let your faith be your guide,
        raising humanity---your cause,
        Some days filled with accomplishments,
        Some days filled with regrets.
        Some days we'll always remember.
        Some days we can never forget.

Ol' Blue

I was just a baby, when my dad bought his truck.
A Ford F-150, Carolina blue for good luck.

Worked her hard on the farm, nothing she could not do.
Spent a week thinking of names, settled on "Ole' Blue."
　　Sometimes your wheels have meaning,
　　They've grown old just like you.

Under the hood were 300 horses, eight-foot bed in back.
Four on-the-floor, 8-ball shifter, rear window 6-gun rack.

That truck was always with us, it never let us down.
She'd ride the fields all week long, and clean-up for church in town.
　　Sometimes your wheels have meaning,
　　They've grown old just like you.
　　They're faded, frayed and rusted,
　　But it's still the same Ole' Blue.

The day I turned 16, Daddy tossed me those keys.
"Treat her right" he said,
"she's been a good friend to me."

Some nights I'd get lost,
on the wrong side of town.
I don't know how she'd do it,
but she'd get me home safe and sound.
　　Sometimes your wheels have meaning,
　　They've grown old just like you.
　　They're faded, frayed and rusted,
　　But it's still the same Ole' Blue.

The Hammer

Just off the job,
Day hot as hell.
Yanking off my boots,
Can see my feet swell.
Used to own the company,
Building the dream home,
Now I'm just a laborer,
Doing what I'm told.

      Don't matter if you own the hammer,
      Or if you are only swinging it,
      Don't ever let the bank get hold,
      Or surely, you'll get hit.

Pulling my 12-hour shift,
On site at 7:00 sharp,
Humping straight through lunch,
Super's on the march.
Half the work ain't done right,
Jackleg, is standard fare,
Soon as the super is out of sight,
No one really cares.

      Sad, the world we live in,
      Good folks getting screwed,
      Stretching for the American Dream,
      Only to be cut in two.

         Don't ever put down that hammer,
         make each stroke strong and true,
         steady the beat, blow by blow,
         for the power is within you.

Sad Country Song

At work they cut my hours,
Saving money, cutting my health plan.
But I don't make enough to eat,
While they pay big bonuses to the man.

I'm praying for some help,
All my buddies in the same boat.
We're all just four weeks from the street,
Just barely staying afloat.

My wife just skipped a period,
Mounds of bills, I can't pay.
The world is kicking my ass,
I live a sad country song every day.

Today, there is no normal,
World is upside down.
Rules have changed forever,
Walls are tumbling down.

My son, he just asked me,
Why I never seem to smile.
I can't bring myself to tell him,
We'll lose the farm in just a while.

It seems we've lost our way;
We're ripping at the seams.
Are we witnessing the end
of the American Dream?

The values that built this country,
Are surely alive today.
We must all stand together,
To protect the American Way.

Our strength is in our people,
Who share a common faith.
Who look with love upon their neighbor,
And stand up for the American Way.

Fight And Pray

What do you do with idle time?
When you've been laid-off, there are no dry eyes,
We'll lose the house, it just ain't right,
But I can't stand proud with idle time.

What do you do with the memories?
A life now gone, staring back at me,
I've worked so hard, it hurts to fall,
But I'm not done yet, and I'll still stand tall.
  Fight and Pray,
  Fight and Pray.
  We remain.

Where are our leaders, in all this mess?
Making promises, they'll soon forget,
Passing laws, we will all regret,
Whose fighting for us, the table is set.

There's a founding document in some D.C. drawer,
That our current leaders choose to ignore,
Many people died to gain these rights,
I think my friend, it's time to fight.
  Fight and Pray
  Fight and Pray,
  We Remain.

People they always see the truth,
The American Way, it's bulletproof,
Let's stand together one and all,
Saving our Great Country from the fall.
  Fight and Pray
  Fight and Pray,
  We Remain.

House of Cards

A big degree,
from an Ivy league school,
Pimping for the "too big to fail",
money makes the rules.

Math majors all the way,
lose the slide rule,
hanging in the King's castle,
waiting to steal the jewels.

Using complexity and confusion,
you can fool them all,
Always right, not a chance,
there is no crystal ball.
Our world is a balloon,
a small prick will pop it.
A house of cards,
a slight wind will drop it.

Sheepskin hanging on the wall,
6 zeroes of debt to buy it,
Ten-thousand-dollar client nights,
man, you should try it.

Fear and risk,
a very profitable potion,
Truth, integrity,
sadly, dying notions.

Where did all the substance go,
now it's all style.
Screw the working man on the corner,
while sporting a wise-ass smile.

    Our world is a balloon,
    a small prick will pop it.
    A house of cards,
    an ill-wind will drop it.

Walk on by,
with your head held high,
You'll miss the small prick,
or the ill wind, gathering nearby…

The balloon is about to pop,
 long way to the ground.
House of cards falling, citizens screaming - - -
leaders hear no sound.

    .

Awaken

The words a con,
Restrain the soul,
Just flash a smile,
Show some gold.

You're not a being,
You're a nine-digit ID,
A cog in the system,
Just another currency.

The degrees a sham,
Don't really need,
Debt now planted,
Long slow bleed.

Dull the mind,
Disconnect the heart,
Dumb down the masses,
That's where it starts.

Medicate daily,
You choose your pill,
From clarity to haze,
You know the drill.

Career is a joke,
We'll tell you when to stand,
Mindless repetition,
It's part of the plan.

The mind now blown,
The heart now stone,
The masses now one,
We're almost done.

> Awaken the mind,
> Connect the heart,
> Awaken the masses,
> It's not too late to start.

> > A dollar sign,
> > stamped on your forehead,
> > Government property,
> > quite easily led.

> > > Awaken the mind,
> > > connect the heart,
> > > awaken the masses.
> > > It's not too late to start.

Peace of Mine

They closed the plant on Sunday,
They asked us all to leave.
Blamed it all on overseas,
But we all knew it was greed.

I was a senior worker,
Been there all my life.
They killed us with a paycheck,
Could a' just as well been a knife.

Some days are oh, so precious,
You wish you could stop time.
But in a world filled with heartache,
All I want is peace of mind.

The kids are now all grown,
Don't hear from them at all.
I'm okay, but it really hurts mama,
How hard is it to call?

I lost my love a year ago,
Her heart just finally broke.
Not sure if it was the kids,
Or the cigarettes she smoked.

Some days are oh, so precious
You wish you could stop time.
But in a world filled with heartache,
All I want is peace of mind.

Now my body's falling apart,
My eyes refuse to see.
My ticker's out of rhythm,
Balls hurt when I pee.

They say that it's all natural,
We grow old gracefully.
That sounds pretty good for someone else,
Just please don't let it happen to me.

Some days are oh so precious
You wish you could stop time.
Now fading memories are all I have,
Of a life that was once mine.

Wasted
In
Williamsburg*

Nine Hours to Nashville

I'd never been there, thought about it a lot,
Dreamed of it every night, where I'd get my shot.
All those years a-playing, those Walmart parking lots,
Riding country roads, crashing on a cot.

Words in my head, songs in my heart,
Took all the courage I could muster, just to make a start.
    I'm nine hours from Nashville, had to leave my home,
    Seeing the world along the way, places that I'll roam.

Now I've left the band, trying it on my own,
They'll always be my family, but I had to stand alone,
    I'm five hours from Nashville, lots to think about,
    Rolling hills and farmland, seem to call me out.

Unsure where I'm headed, what the good Lord has in store,
Lots of things I've got to share, knocking at the door.
    I'm two hours from Nashville, and every dream I've ever had.
    Left broken homes and heartaches, just to take my chance.

The spirit is riding with me, many places we will go,
Singing words and notes, to a sold-out Ryman Show.
    I'm one hour from Nashville, can feel it in my bones,
    The world is waiting, future has been sown,
Words in my head, songs in my heart,
I've landed here in Nashville, to make a new start.

Let's Do Another One, We All Don't Know

Gang has come together, it's open mike night.
Waiting on the drummer, he's nowhere in sight.

Lead singer hummin', he's almost ready to go,
Voice sounds like gravel, can sing it just so!

The barmaids are screaming
Hey…we want a show!
Let's do another one,
We all don't know.

Now we're off and rolling, crowd hears the beat.
Straining hard to catch the tune, shuffling their feet.

Lead guitar jumps right in, drummer's close behind.
Singers searching for a clue, a familiar note he can't find.

The barmaids are screaming
Hey…we want a show!
Let's do another one,
We all don't know.

Dive Bar Inn

Used car lots on every side, a tiny parking lot.
People come from miles around, to reach the drive-in spot.

It isn't much to look at, but the beer is good and cold,
All the waitresses are well fed, and the music's solid gold.

Preppies are not welcome! Hell no to Top 40 Hits…
Don't tell me about it, I grew up in shit like this.

The barroom's got character, from years of wear and tear.
Smells that you can't recognize, drinking too many beers to care.

The tables papered with labels, from amber ale to stout.
The local rowdies filing in, to drink, eat and shout.

8-ball in the corner, owner has high score.
Challenge her if you're feeling lucky…win, you're shown the door.

Country folks they go, to a place you need to get…
Trust me, I should know; I grew up in shit like this.

Head Turner

Sitting in a honky-tonk,
Near closing time,
Making love to my Bud,
Just to ease my mind.

Long week is over,
Pulled a double shift,
If I died tomorrow,
I'd be barely missed.

Juke box playing,
Some classic Hank,
Door swings open,
In the head turner came.

She's a real head turner
Something to see,
Only take one night,
To make a man out of me

Long flowing blond hair,
Polka-dot halter top,
Denim jean Daisy Mae's,
All the jaws dropped.

A real head turner,
The place just froze,
Only Hank kept singing,
Cheatin' hearts ought to know.

You're a real head turner,
Total package- - - easy to see,
All I need is a chance,
Show you the man I can be.

She sat down beside me,
Not sure what to do,
Tipped my hat easy like,
Said "how do you do?"

Spent that night together,
Head turner and me,
We both took a chance,
She made a man out of me.

I Just Gotta Know

(Don't Delete Me)

Don't tell me on Twitter,
G-mail I'll pass,
Instagram never,
Internet won't last.

To hell with texting,
I'd rather take a walk,
For God's sakes baby,
Can't we just talk.

> Don't care how you do it,
> Message, text or type,
> I just gotta know,
> Am I part of your life?

Life on a small screen,
Distraction complete,
Glued to your hand,
Just hit delete,

The governments listening,
Russians don't care,
To many connections,
With no time to share.

> Don't care how you do it,
> Message, text or type,
> I just gotta know,
> Do you dream of me each night?

I've fallen for you baby,
You've captured my heart,
A future has begun,
Two joined from the start.

Don't care how you do it,
Message, text or type,
I just gotta know,
Don't it feel right?

Don't care how you do it,
Message, text or type,
I just gotta know,
Will you be my wife?

Now, put down that phone,
And reach for my hand,
Say yes to me baby,
Make me a happy man.

Big City Back Country

She was born in a high rise, I was born in a barn,

She was raised on concrete; I was raised on a farm.

She always had a driver, I'd rather hitchhike,

She's never had a license; I'm glued to my bike.

        She's my big city girl

        I'm a back country boy.

We met at a bar, on our big city tour,

She was dressed to the nines; I was dressed dirt poor.

Faded genes, torn shirt, manly footwear,

Tipped a 10-gallon hat, she couldn't help but stare.

I opened with Howdy, in my slow Texas style,

She didn't say nothin', just offered a smile.

        Now she's my big city Mama,

        And I'm her back country Man.

I offered my hand, soon we would dance,

This back country boy had taken the chance.

We started up fast, and ended up slow,

And hell, she could two-step, what do you know.

        Now she's my big city Mama,

        And I'm her back country Man.

She was born in a high rise, I was born in a barn,

We're mixing big city magic and slow southern charm.

        Now she's my big city Mama,

        And I'm her back country Man.

Got No Shot

The door swings open and in she walks,
Eyes are popping- - -the boys "jaws" drop.

Whole lotta years, since she was in this bar,
A little girl then, she ain't no more.

Stacked on top, with a loaded backend,
She don't know it yet, but I'm her man.
The boys lean over, they know she's hot,
      Twenty to one, you're a long shot.
      Got no shot....got no shot.

Now I'm not your brother, but I am your friend,
Son, this right here, is a match you can't win.

She grabbed her a cowboy and started to dance,
Whole bar was watching...man, I got no chance.
My buddies are howling, she's hot to trot,
      Five to one, you got no shot.
      Got no shot....got no shot.

But I've got something you ain't got,
Just watch and learn while I take my shot.

We hit the dance floor as I grabbed her hand,
Clogging and two stepping to beat the band.

We boot scoot booggied, and she stood by her man,
We both saw the light, until closing time came.

      We kept on moving, gave it one last shot,
      Went off an even money,- - -I took my shot.
      Took my shot....took my shot...

Living it, Loving it, Lakeside

Sun rising over Carolina pines,
  Gliding down the road, boat trails behind,
  Million-dollar day, not a cloud in the sky,
  Just spent a week in hell, just to get lakeside.

  Cooler full of cold ones,
  Bojangles in the box,
  Evan Williams as fuel treatment,
  Just looking for a redneck fox.

        Man, I'm living it, and I'm loving it,
        I've got to get lakeside.

  Don't matter if she's wearing Carolina blue,
  Or N. C. State red,
  I can't see past those Daisy Dukes,
  She's messing with my head.

  Birds go flying by,
  Feathers don't cover much,
  Don't cost nothing to have a look,
  But brother, please don't touch.
  Now she's living it, and boy I'm loving it,
        We've got to get- - -lakeside.

One Last Cast

The water still at first light, morning by the waterside.
Birds stirring as morning calls the new day dawns,

Distant hums become a roar, tourney's started, boats are floored,
Motors wide open, pursue the special fishing hole,
A galloping horse, knight's weapon's his pole,

A record bass,
A coveted prize,
The day just beginning,
The big surprise.

On the hook the secret sauce,
Baited right, now it's all the toss.
Hold your mouth right, line drifts out of sight,
See it before it hits, silence before the strike.

A record bass,
A coveted prize,
The story told over,
Grows in size.

A fight for his life, a fight he can't win,
The netted foe, will be released again.

Chance

Halter top covering,
Someplace I've never seen.
Cut off short shorts,
Where I've never been.

Patches on your pockets,
Looking so cute,
Long legs to match,
Snakeskin cowboy boots.

Walking down the street,
Heads are gonna turn,
Too hot not to watch,
Anytime she could burn.

How could I know her,
What should I say,
Come on macho as hell,
Or the kind, gentler way.

I'm just gonna say it,
"Hello, how are you?"
Or a little more formal,
"How do you do?"

You'd love me if you knew me,
Even though I can't dance,
Not asking for your heart,
Just give this boy a chance.

Now it's years later,
And our love still grows,
Where our lives will take us,
No one really knows.

You know me and you love me,
And you've taught me to dance
I'm asking you to marry me,
Now let's take a chance.

The Chick

The river she coils,
  Moving from wide to tight,
  Cypress trees line the shoreline,
  Knotted fingers reaching for the light.

  Rains from far away,
  Swifter than the eye can see,
  Water flowing in quiet motion,
  Rushing to meet the sea.

  The water's edge is filled with life,
  Spring hatchlings fill the sky,
  Duck broods paddle the shallows,
  Molting feathers, soon they'll fly.

  Spring showers on far away mountains,
  Weaving east from stream to stream,
  Downward rolling always connecting,
  Feeding waves on a distant sea.

  Summer heat brings late afternoon storms,
  Skies angry, from blue to black as night,
  Nature's power on display,
  Heavens with sound and light.

The thunder quickly rolls over,
Yielding water as smooth as glass,
Mirrored horizon water to sky,
A quiet peace restored at last.

Sun nearly lost behind the trees,
Evening sky now gone pink,
White and blues, now orange and gray,
The sun continues to sink.

The first star is sighted,
Night begins to fall,
Air still and water calm,
As the night dawns.

Dark Water

At first my friends were lite,
A golden amber ale.
I'd talk to each one slowly,
At least the first 10 or 12.

It was all part of growing up,
I was finally a man.
Hammering brews with my buddies,
Girlfriends never understand.

Then I dived in darker water,
Whiskey, on the rocks.
Next day was always trouble,
Can't remember what I forgot.

The bottle's not your brother,
Whiskey is not your friend.
Both will lead you to lose it all,
Just you two, in the end.
By now I was married,
She made the perfect wife.
The more I swam in the dark water,
The more I ruined my life.

One day I woke up all alone,
A note beside my bed.
She'd taken the kids and left,
And here's what that note said:

"I am not the perfect wife,

But forgiveness is my friend.

When you raised your hand to me,

I knew that it must end."

The bottle's not your brother,

Whiskey is not your friend.

Both will lead you to lose it all,

Just you two, in the end.

Today, I see every sunrise,

Eyes are clear and bright.

Head is as clean as a mountain stream,

And I pray to God each night.

That my wife might find forgiveness,

Just this one last time.

We'd dive into crystal clear water,

For the rest of our lives.

---

*Special recognition for the Wasted in Williamsburg section goes to my freshman roommate, and living Lafayette High School/William & Mary Football legend, Scott T. Hays, a Williamsburg native. As Freshman, Scott and I had the dubious distinction of posting average weekly BAC levels that were likely significantly higher than our freshman semester GPA. Luckily, our scholarship included summer school so we were able to get the sheepskin in 4 years, fulfilling our mantra "…..2.5 and drive (GPA that is)".

Weeping
In
Williamsburg

Sharon's Way

Child of the Nation, she grew to stand tall.
Challenged in life, she bested them all.

Quiet in person, moving in peace,
As she grew strong, we called her our Chief.

Quick with a smile, heart always sharing,
Giving of her spirit, God knew her as Sharon.

Called as a servant, able to lead,
Whether from the pulpit, or down on her knees.

Seeking the Spirit, in search of her fate,
Guided in life, she dwells in this place.

The great spirit has called her, she has left this space,
Ascended to heaven, seeing God's welcoming face.

The power of God, shown through each of her days,
Blessed to have known her, touched by Sharon's Way.

Dedicated to Sharon Rebecca Bryant, Chief of the Monacan Nation from 2011-2015 (June 22, 1961 – June 23, 2015). A true leader in every sense of the word. As Episcopalian lay minister, Sharon was the first woman chief of the Monacan Nation.

A Mother's Kiss

A mothers' kiss,
A bedtime prayer,
A wish that God,
Would soon be there.

Sleep won't come,
Pictures etched in my mind,
Tears they fall,
God's hard to find.

The liquor flows,
Clouds have formed,
Winds are rustling,
It's about to storm.

A loving voice suddenly sharp,
A hand gets raised,
The blows that follow,
A vow betrayed.

For better or worse,
Not sure I can,
A girl, a mother, a wife,
I don't understand.
He's wounded inside,
Why strike at me,
I'm all he has,
Why can't he see.

I'm leaving he says,
Never to return,
We all hear the threat,
Words that burn.

The breakdown comes,
Blinking through the tears,
The realization of love,
And all that it can bear.

Some risk it all,
Just for a good time,
A lifetime, a family,
All on the line.

The power of a Mother's kiss
It is always there,
The essence of love,
And all that it bears.

Stained

I can't shake the day we said "I do",
Looking back now, I was a fool.
You said "I'll always love you",
But if only then I knew.
It's not what you say,
It's all in what you do.
I saw all the signs,
Screaming danger ahead,
Blinking lights,
All flashing red.

Now our marriage is failing,
There's only pain,
Vows now broken,
A wedding bed stained.
The love we once had,
The life once dreamed.
Torn and tattered,
Ripped at the seams.
I saw all the signs,
Screaming danger ahead,
Blinking lights,
All flashing red.

How could I have missed it,
It was plain as day.
You've never loved me,
Is all I can say.
It's hard to explain,
I weep hearing your name,
Tears and a broken heart,
are all that remain.

Heart in Pain

Moments make the life,
Seconds are sands.

Flipping the hour glass,
Slipping through our hands.

Time spent with others,
The gift meant for all.
Moments we should be giving,
Listening to the call.

The seed never sown, simply remains.
A field never grows, if it has no rain.

Two souls seeking peace,
Not sure where to start.
Open to what might be,
A blending of the heart.

Spirit is creation,
All seeking to be whole.
Joining the heart and mind,
We meet our very soul.

It's hard to be creative...with a mind in chains.
A heart can never be free...when it beats in pain.

Broken Ornaments

The holiday season comes, year after year,
With the promise of giving, but there's no giving here.

A family adrift, in search of a rudder,
A fearful, displaced mother, and a recently failing father.

The days that once brought sunshine, now only bring rain,
The clean and the pure, now permanently stained.

The home we once knew, where boys grew to men,
Stripped from our hands, Your banker is no friend.

Lost are the dreams, plans that seemed to matter,
A life's worth of work, on the floor in tatters.
>What was it worth,
>All the sweat and the tears,
>The blood and the bruises,
>All those lost years.

Is it time to quit, to simply fade away,
To admit that we are nothing, dust floating in the haze?

Drifting on the breeze, untethered in space,
No grounding, no anchor, no sense of place.

A heart ripped open, unsure what happens next,
Extended hands reaching, unsure of what to expect.

Should I reach out, or should I withdraw?
My eyes fill with tears, at the things that I saw.

Shall I even try, the world seems not to care,
It spins on by, like I'm not even there.

Does my life matter? Only to a small few.
A circle closing in on itself, disappears, who knew?

We were dust, before we became,
That same magic mix that made us, surely remains.

Dust we will be again, but not just yet,
My days are not done, my family's sun has not set.

Pain is a teacher, that can harden the heart,
Leading to desperation, tearing families apart.

Love conquers pain, strength to persevere,
Believe when no one else does, God is already here.

    We were dust,
    Before we became,
    That same magic mix that made us
    Surely remains - - - surely remains…

Sliced

The air was as light as a summer breeze,

Until you turned and threw those words at me.

I didn't see them coming,

There was no way I could know.

Emotions that built up inside you,

Bottled inside, barely showed.

Now I'm sliced wide open,

Nearly cut in two,

Completely lost without you.

Was it something I said,

Or did or did not do.

I've never stopped loving you,

Never been untrue.

Lying awake in the dark of the night,

Wishing and hoping I could set things right.

I'm sliced wide open,

Don't know what to do,

Completely lost without you.

My world has receded,

I'm totally alone.

No one cares where I've been,

Or where I've gone.

The air around me, once light as the breeze,

Turns heavy, I'm down on my knees.

I'm sliced wide open,

My heart is split in two.

Lost forever without you.

The Hurt Year

Three brothers standing, shoulder to shoulder, one rests nearby.
Together they bury their father, under a grey fall sky.
The past year has been bruising, a mother, brother and father passed,
Seeking the grace of a loving God, the only thing that lasts.

Weeping for departed souls, never to walk this plane.
Clinging to each other, we are all that remain.
Bound up in sorrow, with bleeding but grateful hearts,
The pain eventually passes, but it has really just started.

The daily gift of presence, often overlooked,
Being in the moment, the chance we never took.
Remembering all a parent gives,
Countless daily gifts each day they live.

Now there's only silence, loving voices that we miss,
Words of comfort won't come, floating on the wind.
Shared lessons learned from lives well lived,
Shoes now unfilled, no life left to give.

Three hands on a casket, one final goodbye,
A body returned to the Earth, spirits joined in the sky.
Surely as he's lowered, we must all rise,
The sun will set today, but tomorrow we must shine.

Dedicated to my Godparents Joyce and Bobby Cournow, and their son Bobby Jr.

The Wall

Rare is the path that is always clear,
Many the minds, clouded with fear.
Certain of nothing, choices are blurred,
Not sure how we got here, future obscured.

Seeking a pattern, cause and effect,
Randomized outcomes, who dares to project.
The experiment proceeds, who is its master,
Are we in control, or headed for disaster?

A collective world, defaulting to "me",
Submerged in self, that's all you see.

Sun rising and setting, based on my needs,
Gratification, consumption, the powers we feed.
Asleep at the wheel, cruising through life,
Cars and kids, a made beautiful wife.

Missing a stop sign, never did brake,
Just hit the wall, may never wake.

Barely making it, holding on tight,
Material security, no longer in sight.
Dust cloud settles, bloody and bruised,
Clinging to each other, new reality fused.

Gone are the things that really don't matter,
Found, the loving bonds we've gathered.
The answer is less, stop reaching for more,
Satisfied and grateful for what life has in store.

Rejoicing in uncertainty, why must we know?
All of the answers or where the dreams go.
Welcome each morning with an open heart,
Each day is a new beginning.....make a good start.

The wall has just kept you from choosing the wrong path,
Be quiet and grateful - - - for all that you have.

Ashes

An idyllic life in some suburban myth,

Burned to the ground, through the ashes we sift.

Little is left of the life they once knew,

Charred remains, completely burnt through.

Walking the rubble, that was once their life,

Sacred vows, holding fast a husband to a wife.

Children grown up, express willful renunciation,

Witnessing daily, society's public castration.

      Why wouldn't they walk---from a game that's rigged.

      Laden with debt…..slop to the pigs.

A government of sell-outs, to the highest bidder they go,

Citizens muted, asleep at the wheel, they never know.

An education scam, mountains of debt- - - no way to pay,

An under-skilled job, just slaving away.

      Lost in the fog, searching for your path,

      The Spirit gets trapped, in all that math.

Tax man comes first, insurance out of sight,

Landlord knocking - - - get the rent right.

      A family heated, forged, twisted and turned,

      A family built on love can't burn.

            Lost in a fog, searching for your path,

            The Spirit gets trapped, in all that math.

                  Keep family at your center, find the God in you.

                  Stir those ashes, watch what love can do.

                        The sky is clearing, you see your way,

                        With love in your heart, seize the day.

Wondering
In
Williamsburg

Where We've Been...
Where Shall We Go?

I am just a poor boy,
Though my story is seldom told …. (Simon and Garfunkel/The Boxer/April
1969)….

1950's

We entered this world post World War II,

First generation to live beside the Nukes.

In the dust just settled, left in a Cold War haze,

Searching for un-American activities, carried the day.

Heavens weaponized as the Sputnik flew,

How long humanity had left, no one really knew.

1960's

At home cities burned, a true societal test,

Centuries of racial discrimination- - -at last put to rest.

The civil rights movement, Jefferson's declaration fulfilled,

At the costs of a seminal leader, whose blood was spilt.

A government of malfeasance, totally run amok,

A crooked leader, and a well-educated band of thugs.

1970's

We get the vote, but have no choices,

Overwhelming nausea, silences our voices.

We hold our noses, and pull the lever,

The lesser of bad choices, can we not do better?

We shoot for the moon and pay big bucks for gas,

What college to choose, this should be a blast!

1980's

Hi-Ho, Hi-Ho, it's off to work we go…

We're really smart now… I hope it shows.

Ours is a government now seeking redemption,

"Tear down this wall" shout world markets in jubilation!

Less government is good, a burgeoning bourgeoisie,

Landing that first job, playground revisited "…pick me….pick me.."

1990's

Enter Slick Willie and the famous cigar,

The continual lowering of the behavioral bar.

The definition of "is" has become a Presidential role,

Monica's the first star in the endless "me-too" show.

Enter impeachment into the American lexicon,

Boys behaving badly- - -all sides are wrong.

2000's

An evil eleven and two buildings, unite us all,

A handful of courageous Americans save the White House from a fall.

Three thousand Patriots perish, yet there is very little blood,

Pulverized to dust, a spiritual rain bringing the coming flood.

Centuries of off-shore activities, known and unknown,

Inspiring deep-seated hatred, the seeds have been sewn.

2010's

A milestone President, the slavery stain removed,

A listing ship of state, guided by an inexperienced and marginal crew.

Subversion of individual accomplishment to "our community should…"

The perversion of society- - - just "do it if it feels good…"

Forget self-enlightenment, too much work- - -no dopamine there,

Choose self-entertainment, no effort- - -distractions to spare.

2020's

Glued to your I-phone, Facebook away!

Before you know it, you've wasted your whole day.

Why not choose silence, enter your sacred space,

The quiet divine heart center, the seat of all grace.

In the clearing stands a boxer,
And a fighter by his trade,
And he carries the reminders,
Of every glove that laid him down,
Or cut him as he cried out
(The Boxer-Closing Verse/Simon and Garfunkel)

Who's to know what comes next,

Or the challenges the world might bring.

The only question we need answer:

Are we on the sidelines, or are we in the ring?

What is a Man?

What is a man? And who defines him…
Is it his time? Or the time that is behind him.
Is it his actions? Or is it his words?
What he accomplishes, or the people he serves?

I guess one day, I'll be a man,
And I'll know what that means.
I'll see where I'm going,
And I'll know where I've been.

Is he his children? A husband to a wife,
A son or a brother, all the roles of his life.
Is he his toys? Things that he gathers,
The houses, cars, and boats. Are these the things that matter?

Is he his money? His rolled-up net worth.
Add up all them zero's, don't equal one kind word.
Is work who he is, what he gives himself to.
At his center what remains? Are we really what we do?

I think that in the end,
A man is all these things.
And that in the blending of his life,
True inner peace springs.

Open

An open hand, a clenched fist,

An open mind, an opinion fixed,

An open door, the status quo.

  If steps aren't taken, you'll never know.

A world passing by, but yet so close,

Most don't even see it, too blind to know,

The God inside them, will never show.

  If the heart is not opened, you'll never know.

Snared in a trap, the world calls normal,

Living only to work, a life gone graphic,

Desperation in black and white, foes always come at night.

  If the mind's not open, you'll never know.

Colours of life, faded to shades of grey,

Going through the motions, the acts that we play,

  Energy draining fast, clinging to a distant past.

Seek the God in all you meet, in what you do and say,

Burning pages of yesterday, illuminates the future way.

  Take the steps, open your heart,

  Unlock your mind, you must do your part.

  Take the steps, open your heart,

  Unlock your mind, make a new start.

The Stream of Life

Streaming past the grey stone rocks,
The river flows, eternity passing.
A singular flow, forced to split,
Quiet calm that yields without splashing.

Broken rock forged a millennium ago,
Thrown together, haphazard it seems.
Now creates the thundering sound,
As the river across it streams.

Listless flow once silent and steady,
Now agitated to sound and spray.
Deep channels forced to flatten out,
And meet the light of day.

The river like life itself,
Can seem to barely move.
The surface hiding all within,
The losses, trials and truths.

The sudden drops of life will come,
There's little we can do.
We find ourselves falling fast,
Questioning all we thought we knew.

The shallows will soon follow,
As the rocky bottom we walk.
Ever mindful of the few things we can carry,
Not sure of all things in life we've sought.

With rapid changes around us,
Loud noise at every turn.
Be choiceful what you gather,
And what you need to burn.

The flow of life can seem random,
Over flat and rocky paths.
Our choice is what we cling to,
Souvenirs from a distant past.

Our souls are like the rivers,
Flowing, bending, never to yield.
Deep and shallow, thin and wide,
Slow and fast, silent and loud.

Soon as sound and fury leave us,
The calm of life remains.
What you've lost, you never needed,
What you've gained, you can't explain.

Monican Mountain Morning

A foundation rock,
A cascading stream,
A seat of souls.
On the Spirit rolls.

The totem pole silent,
Looks down on this place.
The rocks in the stream bed,
Symbolizing each Nation members face.

Quiet beneath the water,
Unable to speak.
For four hundred years,
Their Nation they seek.

　　The land is their brother,
The water is their friend.
To live in perfect harmony,
　　Is to have a good end.

To live from the spirit,
Is the Monacan way.
To be one, to be all,
In all our relations.

The people were hunted,
Their name a disgrace.
The State and the white man,
An ancient Nation displaced.

But the Spirit still lives,
On this quiet mountainside.
Where the People still walk,
Arm in arm, side by side.

The land is their brother,
The water is their friend.
To live in perfect harmony,
Is to have a good end.

And the sun will soon rise,
On a nation reborn.
On a restored homeplace,
Whose Spirit is strong.

Who again will walk proudly,
Their heads held high.
In thanks for the Mother,
Eyes raised to Father Sky.

In the East will be life,
In the South the bright sky.
In the West the horizon,
In the North the Nation's rise.

Dedicated to the Monacan Indian Nation 7/2009

Joined

Newlyweds saying yes, two becoming one.
Families enjoined, under God's shining spring sun.

Bound to the promise, of what can be.
When you lose yourself, and discover the We.

Seeking the best in all you love, what we are called to do.
God whose spark created us all, is surely aflame in you.

Sharing our love with another is our greatest gift.
Two now joined as one burning bright, the spirit lifts.

Mirrors

The crystal blue sky, bordered in pink,
A mirrored world,
A sun rises as the moon sinks.

A haloed sun breaks over the pines,
Millions of days gone,
But this day is mine.

A warming sun, the morning broken,
A million giving rays,
A giving God has spoken.

A sun fully risen, calling my name
Strikes me with a sun beam,
I'll never be the same.

The world reflects you,
Are you shining bright?
Mirrors surround you,
Won't you be the light?

The Seed

Wind whistling through the trees,
Spirit moving as nature.
Nudging the seed, it falls from a limb,
Into the stream it lands.

The rushing current grabbing hold,
The clear invisible hand.
Down the stream the seed rushes,
Dancing atop the flow.

A new world rushing by,
On to destinations unknown.
Soon the stream empties,
Into the wandering creek.

Seemingly without movement,
It carves out the deep.
The water moves more slowly,
With quiet power and grace.

Seeming almost to be still,
Ripples etched across its face.
Still dancing atop the moving water,
Bouncing as the waves hit the shore.

Lost to the wind and water,
Not knowing what is in store.
Inside the seed unchanged,
Nature waits to see God's plan.

To release its full potential,
With the help of sun and sand.
The creek, it meets the river,
Water great and wide.

The seed still riding,
No place it can hide.
At last the seed it catches,
The wind and wave it seeks.

Splashing onto the life-giving shores,
Life rushing to break free.
Pressure builds at its center
Sun baking its outer shell.

All our hopes and dreams.
Spirit guides the swell,
Soon life bursting forth.
World suddenly opens wide.

Roots weaving into earth,
Shoots aiming to reach the sky.
Air, soil, water and sun,
Nature's love is all we need.

See nature in all man,
We are all just seeds.
Sometimes we float,
Sometimes we drift.

Where we'll land,
We can't know.

The Portrait

The portrait hangs on the family room wall.
Above a fieldstone fireplace, where I burned it all.
The floor is covered with spent embers and ash.
All that remains of a life that has passed.
The pictures and letters, the gifts that you gave.
The symbols of love, your heart says to save.
Now into the flame, the pieces of our past.
A collection of things, but our love will last.
This door that we close, the path that we chose,
We'll walk together, where, only God knows.

This room filled with spirits, always full of our friends.
Where family came together, to love, heal and mend.
This room full of joy, our family life spent.
From wedding to wake, all heaven sent.
This room full of sadness, holding each other we cried.
For dashed hopes and friends lost, with God by our side.
This room now empty, save the ash on the floor.
A home now just a house, when we walk through that door.

Our family is smiling, our future is bright,
Our faith is our compass, our God is our sight.

Full Cup

You call tales, I call heads,
You like to turn-in early, I won't go to bed.

You're always holding on, I'm always letting go,
You have to have all the answers, I say "hell I don't know..."
      I used to be half empty,
      But now I've got a full cup.

      You like to row your boat, I'm content to just float.
      You like riding highways, I love a country road.

      You want to go fast, when we should take it slow,
      I never ask why? You've always got to know.

         I used to be half empty,
         Now, I've got a full cup,

         We've got a full cup.
         Full Cup.

Prayer of Possibility

(100 Words to Start Everyday)

Lord,

We come before you today with capable hands, open minds and grateful hearts. Thankful for the gifts and talents you have given us, knowing we must use these in service of our fellow man.

We ask Lord, that your Holy Spirit dwell among us as we share our lives and life energy today and every day - - - inspire us to good and great things, as we know:

-Only one life, that soon is passed, only things done with Love will lasts.

We ask these things praising your Son, Our Savior Jesus Christ, with and in Him all things are possible.

Remembering

Inspiration is a gift from God, freely flowing from the Universal Mind, to the connected Individual Soul.

Creation is of the hand of Man, ancient vision becoming today's reality, your actions carry the day. Carpe Diem….

Wishing That...

Someday, somewhere – anywhere, unfailingly, you'll find yourself, and that and only that, can be the happiest or bitterest hour of your life.

-Pablo Neruda

Photo credit detail**:

Waking
Christopher Wren Building,
W&M Campus

Working
The Blacksmith Shop,
Colonial Williamsburg

Wasted
The Stockade on Duke of Gloucester Street

Weeping
Bruton Parish Church
on Duke of Gloucester Street

Wondering
Chownings' Tavern
on Duke of Gloucester Street

Writing
Thomas Jefferson Statue

on DOG Street, gazing across campus at the
Wren building. I wonder were he here today,
what pray tell he would be thinking/writing?

Behind the Pen and Ink

Gray Oliver was born in Williamsburg at Bell Hospital, on June 8th 1956. His family moved from Williamsburg to the west end of Richmond, Virginia in the middle of 1958. He and his brothers Al (older) and Erick (younger) grew up in what was Henrico County's fast developing west end, all graduating from Douglas Freeman High School.

In the fall of 1973, Gray was offered and accepted a full scholarship to play football and baseball at William & Mary, where he was on campus from 1974-1978, graduating in June, with a major in Government and a Religion minor.

Following his graduation, Gray was offered a career with Procter & Gamble. After accepting the offer, he worked for 25 years as a senior executive in roles all over the Southeastern states, eventually returning to Richmond in August of 1994 with his family.

Following his career with Procter & Gamble, Gray split his time between consulting/mentoring and writing, also finding time to coach on several local junior high and little league sports teams.

He and his wife, Cynthia live in Richmond, while their three sons and a daughter are currently scattered all over the 50 states, from east coast to west coast with one in Hawaii.

through the years

Thoughts/Comments/Questions/Suggestions/Speaking Requests?

We would Love To Hear Them!

Reach Gray at GNOTSM@GMAIL.COM or via

Phone 804.350.1689

Special thanks to the talented management staff at CQP&P especially Patricia Palmour and Cynthia Marie Cornett, for lending us their editing prowess as the final press first edition was completed and readied for publishing.

Poems Listing By Theme

Poems Listing By Theme

More Walking in Williamsburg resources

Resource	Website
Walking In Williamsburg Website	walkinginwilliamsburg.com

College of William and Mary	wm.edu
Colonial Williamsburg	colonialwilliamsburg.org
Busch Gardens	buschgardens.com
Water Country	watercountryusa.com
Williamsburg Inn	www.colonialwilliamsburghotels.com